Dan Bongino Fired: Why Fox News Lost Its Star Commentator

By

Gregory D. Richardson

Copyright

Table of Contents

Chapter 1: Inside the Mind of Dan Bongino - A Profile of His Life and Beliefs

Dan Bongino is a former Secret Service agent, conservative commentator, and Republican politician who has been a prominent figure in American politics and media for the past decade. Born on December 4, 1974, in Queens, New York, Bongino has had a diverse career that has included law enforcement, politics, and media.

Early Life and Education

Dan Bongino was born and raised in Queens, New York, where he grew up in a working-class family. His father was a New York City sanitation worker, while his mother worked as a waitress. Bongino attended Queens College, where he earned a bachelor's degree in psychology in 1997. While in college, Bongino was a member of the college's fencing team and was also involved in the Reserve Officer Training Corps (ROTC).

After graduating from college, Bongino began his career in law enforcement, joining the New York City Police

Department (NYPD) in 1995. He worked as a police officer for several years, including a stint in the NYPD's elite Street Crime Unit, which was disbanded in the wake of the Amadou Diallo shooting.

Secret Service Career

In 1999, Bongino joined the United States Secret Service, a federal law enforcement agency tasked with protecting the President, Vice President, and other high-level officials. Bongino was initially assigned to the agency's New York Field Office, where he worked on a variety of cases, including financial crimes and identity theft.

In 2002, Bongino was selected to join the Presidential Protection Division (PPD), the Secret Service's elite unit responsible for protecting the President and his family. Bongino was initially assigned to the protective detail for President George W. Bush and later worked on the protective details for President Barack Obama.

Bongino's time in the Secret Service was not without controversy. In 2012, he was investigated by the agency's Office of Professional Responsibility (OPR) for leaking information to the media about a Secret Service prostitution scandal that occurred during the President's visit to Cartagena, Colombia. Bongino denied the allegations and was ultimately cleared of any wrongdoing.

Political Career

After leaving the Secret Service in 2011, Bongino decided to pursue a career in politics. In 2012, he ran for Congress in Maryland's 6th congressional district, which encompasses parts of Montgomery, Frederick, and Washington counties. Bongino ran as a Republican in a heavily Democratic district and ultimately lost to the incumbent, Democrat John Delaney.

Undeterred, Bongino ran again for the same seat in 2014, but again was defeated by Delaney. In 2016, Bongino decided to run for the U.S. Senate in Maryland, but he failed to win the Republican nomination, which was ultimately won by Kathy Szeliga.

Bongino's political career was marked by his conservative views and his support for limited government, fiscal conservatism, and Second Amendment rights.

Media Career

While Bongino was not successful in his political bids, he has been very successful in his media career. In 2015, he began hosting a conservative podcast called "The Renegade Republican," which later became "The Dan Bongino Show." The podcast quickly gained a large following and became one of the most popular conservative podcasts in the country.

In 2018, Bongino joined Fox News as a contributor and commentator. He cemented his status as a conservative media personality with his sharp and passionate commentary on a variety of political issues. Bongino also appeared on other Fox News programs, including "Hannity" and "Fox & Friends."

In 2019, Bongino launched a new podcast called "The Dan Bongino Show," which quickly became one of the most popular podcasts in the country. The podcast features Bongino's commentary on a variety of political issues, as well as interviews with prominent conservative figures.

Bongino has also authored several books, including "Life Inside the Bubble: Why a Top-Ranked Secret Service Agent Walked Away from It All" and "Spygate: The

Attempted Sabotage of Donald J. Trump." Both books were bestsellers and cemented Bongino's status as a prominent conservative voice.

Personal Life

Dan Bongino is married to Paula Andrea Bongino, whom he met while working in law enforcement. The couple has two daughters together and currently resides in Florida. Bongino is a devout Catholic and has spoken publicly about his faith, including his opposition to abortion.

Bongino has also been open about his struggles with health issues. In 2015, he was diagnosed with Hodgkin's lymphoma, a type of cancer that affects the lymphatic system. He underwent treatment and announced in 2016 that he was cancer-free. In 2020, Bongino revealed that he had been diagnosed with a rare form of spinal cancer, which he said had a good prognosis.

In addition to his media and political work, Bongino is also involved in various philanthropic and charitable endeavors. He has worked with organizations such as the Wounded Warrior Project and the Leukemia and Lymphoma Society to raise money for research and support for veterans and cancer patients.

Conclusion

Dan Bongino's personal and professional life is a testament to his dedication to public service and his conservative principles. From his early career in law enforcement to his time in the Secret Service and his political and media career, Bongino has always been a passionate advocate for limited government, individual liberty, and conservative values.

While his political career has not been as successful as he may have hoped, his media career has taken off, and he has become one of the most prominent conservative voices in the country. With his sharp and passionate commentary, Bongino has been able to reach a large audience and influence the national conversation on a variety of political issues.

Despite his success, Bongino has remained grounded and committed to his family, his faith, and his philanthropic work. His personal and professional life is a testament to his commitment to service and his unwavering dedication to his beliefs.

Chapter 2: Why Dan Bongino Left Fox News and What It Means for Conservative Media

Dan Bongino, a prominent media personality, and right-wing commentator revealed his resignation from Fox News during a Thursday podcast broadcast.

Even though the news was unexpected, Bongino insisted that there is no "acrimony" and that the breakup was the product of unsuccessful contract talks.

Fox News and well-known right-wing radio and television broadcaster Dan

Bongino have dissolved their collaboration after 10 years, Bongino revealed on his podcast on Thursday. This week, just before a defamation trial was about to begin, Fox News settled with Dominion Voting Systems for $787 million.

The fiery Trump supporter formerly hosted the Fox News programs "Unfiltered" and "Canceled in the USA."

There is no "big conspiracy theory" or "acrimony," he said on his podcast on Thursday, adding that he had already left the network.

A somber-looking Bongino said, "Unfortunately, last week was my last show on Fox News Channel."

It was difficult to conclude the concert last week. I'll make you a promise: it's not some huge conspiracy theory. There is no hostility... We just weren't able to agree on an extension. He said, "That's really it."

"I had a lot of fun there." For 10 years, they were beneficial to me. A dark day has come. I don't want you to believe they showed me the door; they did offer me the chance to do one farewell concert. But I decided it was better to proceed in this manner for the time being. That's on me, not them.

The host said once again that Fox had given him the chance to do one farewell show this weekend, but he had turned it down.

This Saturday's Bongino show will be replaced by Fox News anchor Lawrence Jones' program, "Lawrence Jones Cross Country." According to the network, a new schedule will be revealed in the next few weeks.

The Saturday at 9 p.m. Eastern time slot of Bongino's program was a hit for the network. The last episode was the day's highest-rated primetime program with 1.18 million viewers.

With 1.3 million viewers and 134,000 viewers in the key demographic, Unfiltered was the most-watched program during primetime on Saturday.

90% of the time, "We were the number one show." Bongino said, "We had a fantastic squad. You'll read a thousand left-wing stories about rubbish, but I can assure you that it's all made up based on my reputation. The only thing involved is a straightforward contract. That is the extent of the complexity.

Fox News sent well wishes for their former anchor in a statement: "We appreciate Dan's contributions and wish him luck in his future endeavors," the statement reads.

Following Fox News's $787 million settlement with Dominion Voting Systems in a slander lawsuit, the Bongino split occurred.

The timing of the separation, according to Bongino, is not ideal in terms of optics.

A defamation lawsuit about the network's coverage of the 2020 presidential election was avoided earlier this week when Fox News agreed to pay Dominion Voting Systems $787.5 million in an eleventh-hour settlement.

In a $1.6 billion lawsuit against the network, Dominion claimed that Fox News had repeated conspiracies about Donald Trump's loss to Joe Biden.

In a press conference, Dominion attorney Justin Nelson said that Fox is paying $787,500,000 to resolve the defamation action, a sum that he claims "represents vindication and accountability."

He said, "Lies have repercussions."

The presenter recognized the optics were poor but urged his viewers to disregard reports that his departure was "acrimonious" or related to the recent Dominion Voting Systems settlement.

The network released the following statement: "We are glad to have resolved our issue with Dominion Voting Systems. We accept the Court's decisions declaring certain assertions about Dominion to be untrue.

This agreement demonstrates Fox's ongoing commitment to the highest journalistic standards. We're hoping that by choosing an amicable settlement with Dominion over the bitterness of a contentious trial, we can help the nation move beyond these problems.

The settlement arrangement prevented what most observers believed would have been a devastating trial for the network, during which owner Rupert Murdoch and primetime personalities like Tucker Carlson and Sean Hannity would have been required to testify in front of a judge.

Dominion is now pursuing legal action against Newsmax, a right-wing media outlet, as well as Trump associates Rudy

Giuliani, Sidney Powell, and Mike Lindell.